chains

also by Ngozi Olivia Osuoha

The Transformation Train
Letter to My Unborn
Sensation
Tropical Escape (with Amos O. Ojwang')
Fruits from the Poetry Planet
Poetry Grenade
Whispers of the Biafran Skeleton

chains

poems by
Ngozi Olivia Osuoha

Poetic Justice Books & Arts
Port Saint Lucie, Florida

©2018/2019 Ngozi Olivia Osuoha

book design and layout: SpiNDec, Port Saint Lucie, FL
cover image: *The Dark Passage* [detail], Kris Haggblom

All rights reserved.

No part of this book may be used or reproduced in any manner whatsoever without written permission except in the case of brief quotations embodied in critical articles and reviews. Members of educational institutions and organizations wishing to photocopy any of the work for classroom use, or authors, artists and publishers who would like to obtain permission for any material in the work, should contact the publisher.

Published by Poetic Justice Books
Port Saint Lucie, Florida
www.poeticjusticebooks.com

ISBN: 978-1-950433-19-3

10 9 8 7 6 5 4 3 2

*for the victims of slavery
and human trafficking*

chains

table of contents

Sabotage Our Enemy Friend	3
The Barbaric Chains of Culture	6
The Palace of a Gorilla	8
Mystery of the Snail	10
Cause Us to Yell	11
Abundant	12
The Place We Neutralize	13
A Whore	14
Milder	15
The Muster	16
Longer	17
The Music	18
The Heathen	20
Uncle Probe	21
He Is Pregnant	22
Brother South Sudan	23
Festival of Rape	24
The Desperate Migrant	26
The Mississippi Slave	28
Fallow	29
The Government	30
ABCD	32
Similar Difference	34
Brainwashed	36
The Irony	38
Marriage Nothing but a Responsibility	39
A Manager	41
Return Young Chibok	42
Help Dear Lord	43

Goodluck	44
There Is God	45
Heed	46
Listen	47
Hearken	48
Lean On the Rock	49
Stay Alert	50
The Boundary	51
No Kicking Like a Ball	52
Some Toke	53
Never You Be Sold	54
Home	55
Nature	56
Chains	57
Slavery	58
Greed	59
Hate	60
Humanity	61
about the author	63

chains

Sabotage Our Enemy Friend

Your smile is unique
A very dirty technique
Your words sound serious
However, highly dangerous,
Your gestures are luring
But the outcome, too boring
Sabotage; our enemy-friend.

You killed your niece
Wrote her a golden piece
You raped your daughter
Saddened, your heart; laughter
Sent your son on suicide
Accused us of genocide,
Sabotage; our enemy-friend.

You preach Justice
And water injustice
You murdered the farmer
Executed the hunter,
Jailed the palm wine tapper
For him not to be a rapper,
Sabotage, our enemy-friend.

You assassinated your opponent
To win the argument,
You visited his widow
And promised open window
That was some camouflage

You actually wanted her as badge,
Sabotage, our enemy-friend

You never from the front
Always altering your font
Shooting from behind
A hard and bitter mind,
You are such a coward
Stupid, insane and wayward
Sabotage, our enemy-friend.

You made your fish a nun
Gave the rat a gun
Ordained your pot, a monk
Caused the kitchen to sink,
Poisoned the bone
Threw it like stone,
Sabotage, our enemy-friend

You are the leader
Yet harsh on gender,
You are the father
You destroyed the ladder,
You are the coach
Messing like cockroach,
Sabotage, our enemy-friend

Strong and resilient
Fit for government,

Bold and courageous
Eager and anxious
Great and sound
But us, you bound,
Sabotage, our enemy-friend

What a shame
What a frame
You instigated enmity
Stained the dynasty,
Crushed our pride
Just for your ride,
Sabotage, you are a disgrace.

The Barbaric Chains Of Culture

There is a stranger
Who buys children
He sells ginger
As religion to men

Come, buy my son
Give me a little food
Wear me a light cotton
And cut off the hood

There is a man
With many wives
He placed a ban
On his people's lives

Tomorrow, when I die
Do not kill a cow
Tie men, women also tie
Bury them alive and bow

There is a rich king
With many concubines
His signet and ring
Are made of bloody-wines

His palace is full of skulls
His robes; human skeletons
Women; his shopping mall
And virgins; his buttons

There is a poor widow
Her home is demolished
Compounding her sorrow
Her farmland is washed

There is a river
That welcomes babies
There is a lover
That murders ladies.

The Palace of a Gorilla

Written boldly on the gate
Welcome to my sacred estate,
Scattered here and there
Gold, silver, everywhere,
The palace of a gorilla

It is a physical paradise
Deceives not the wise,
Because every midnight
Someone loses his sight,
The palace of a gorilla

Young maidens become dogs
Able-bodied men turn frogs,
Behind the covenant
Is a disgusting remnant,
The palace of a gorilla

Turn by turn, they appear
Stage by stage, they disappear
One by one, they tie
Each by each, they die,
The palace of a gorilla

At the middle of the compound
Scores buried, never found
Under the gorilla's bed
Spirit are richly fed,
The palace of a gorilla

Behind his wardrobe
Are youths locked in globe
Beside his resting place
Are elders without face,
The palace of a gorilla

His sandals are destinies
His beads are horror litanies
His bracelet is babies
And his crown, ladies
The palace of a gorilla

Humans line up on the walls
They carry the pillars and post,
Humans, they play like balls
Hidden graves haunt them
The palace of a gorilla

The palace of a gorilla
Built with every molar
Founded on each premolar
Raised up to the solar
The palace, loyalty and royalty

Mystery of the Snail

Following the rail
To deliver a mail
Without any nail
And none to bail
An escape from jail
In the midst of hail
Making a slow sail
With an unnoticed tail,
Trying not to wail
And also not to fail
For all things are frail
And a turbulent grail,
Arrival; MYSTERY OF THE SNAIL

Cause Us to Yell

May we do excel
Inside the cell
And ring like bell
Outside the well,
May the trees we fell
Save us from hell
That all we sell
Shall help us dwell
For us not to swell
Nor offensively smell,
Though we become a jell
May we help quell
And cover the dell
That the truth we tell
Shall cause us to yell

Abundant

The sky is blue
The land is green
The space is large
The future is broad
The faith is great
The vision is clear
The zeal is drunk
The mercy is peak
The dream is big,
And the grace is ABUNDANT

The Place We Neutralize

A world of choice
With some dish of rice,
A life of price
Looking a bit nice,
A walk of prize
Depending on your size,
A coach of dice
Filled with lice
A dream of service,
By the apprentice
A world of short notice
With a whole lot of vice
Where men terrorize,
And women generalize
Where youths commonize
And deeply socialize,
The territory we monetize
And the place we neutralize

A Whore

With the rags she wore
She was kind to the core,
And had a dirty sore
Around her tiny pore;
Enough pain in store
Yet they had her to gore
An ugly shock, a fore
They took her, on shore
With the child she bore
Raped them offshore
And turned her a whore

Milder

If it is a wonder
Then you must ponder
If you have to wander
Put nothing asunder,
If you are a pretender
You cannot be a mender,
Because being a minder
Makes one a reminder
Hence, you may not look yonder
But one must be a bender
For him to get the sender
Be if necessary, a fender
And inevitably a defender
For closing the folder
Can lead to murder
Except you are a welder
Who understands issues tender
And solve each milder

The Muster

Whether it is Easter
Or a new semester,
You can be the truster
And not a monster
Though you are a spinster
You can be a sprinter
Instead of a splinter
And much softer
Though you are shorter
If your heart is lighter
Then make it the roaster
And send it to your sister
Teach her daughter
And save them from slaughter
That there may be laughter
At the muster

Longer

Life can be bigger
It can also be smaller,
If you are humbler
You can be nobler,
If you are homelier
You can be happier,
If you are darker
You may not be safer,
If it is easier
Then it may be cheaper
If you are taller
You may be angrier
If you are an officer
You can lose your muffler
And then greatly suffer,
That is the offer
Which drags it longer

The Music

If you through the Pacific
It will be very hectic
For a picnic
That is the logic,
Though you are romantic
You may not join the titanic
Despite who you mimic
And the power of your magic,
If you are a fanatic
And purely dogmatic
Someday, it turns dramatic
And totally traumatic,
No matter your basic
The statistic
And logistic
It may not be comic
As they point tragic
And deeply barbaric
With a sense of cosmetic
Boiling down to nature, Adamic
Turning demonic
And satanic,
Appearing magnetic
And antagonistic
Then no cleric
No matter how historic
Can make it too classic
Be him democratic
Or autocratic

Or even systematic
Though he is angelic
If he cannot frolic
Then you face the music

The Heathen

In the days, olden
There was a garden
Called Eden
More beautiful than Sweden
There, everything was given
It was like heaven
Nothing was hidden
Except a fruit, forbidden
An order they should hearken
But they misbehaved like children,
Chased it like chicken
Lay with the hen
Broke God's pen,
And turned it a den,
Their spirit was not quicken
For the urge they could not deaden
That, made God redden
So they were far driven
And became sicken,
For life turned wooden
As they worshipped the image; graven
They went harden and harden
And finally like the heathen

Uncle Probe

Welcome uncle probe
Where have you been?
I knew you from teen
With your long sweeping robe.

Welcome uncle probe
Sweep the carpet
Clean the cobweb
Flush them not in the toilet

Uncle probe check the rug
Stop the hug and bug
As a super actor
How much were you paid?

Your finger is here
Your footprint is there,
You have a network
Block and rock.

Before I was born
You have been stealing corn,
You planted everywhere; thorn
And break rising horn.

(BIASED UNCLE...)

He Is Pregnant

Protruding daily
Boldly desperate
Bluntly heavy
Hatching fate

Pushing to deliver
Deeply in trivial
Fake pregnancy or real
Children or quiver

One or twins,
Triplets or quadruplets,
Stillbirth or cripple
Deaf or dumb

Where are the kinsmen?
Buy now your balm
Await unpredictable children
Do not be calm

Where are the women?
Buy tubers of yams
Okporoko and uda
Utazi, uziza and nchonwu
Ose and mkpurumoshosho

He is pregnant
With a covenant,
He is a giant
Expect no ant

YES HE IS PREGNANT....I KNOW

Brother South Sudan

Dear younger brother
Hear the mind of mother,
You have had enough
And tasted all rough,
If you destroy the mosque
You would settle for the kiosk,
If you burn the church
You would sell your torch.

Child soldier, civilian casualty
Burnt school, destroyed home
Young widow, single parent
War, anger, rape
Poverty, famine, hunger, starvation,
Heap of the dead
Diseases; spread

Enough of the ethnic cleansing
Enough of the religious sacrifice,
Ask your eldest brother, Nigeria
Look at your one, Liberia
Find out from Somalia
Watch South Africa
And immediate Sudan
All count still their losses

Festival of Rape

Girlhood is naturally divine
Spinsterhood is not a profession,
Widowhood is not a choice
Womanhood is not a crime

Feminism is a right
Freedom is a right
Stardom, not by rape
Martyrdom, not by scrape

Once a medical student
Was to be a doctor,
Raped like a rodent
Grilled in a sector

He was not remorseful
Even blamed her,
Never was he shameful
Neither was his peer

A festival of rape?
Young, green and minor
Ripped off her shape
Terror and horror

Bold and barbaric culture
Blind, humiliating order
Timid and violent nature
Undignifying our gender

All the movies I see
They showcase love,
Dance! Dance! Dance!
A festival of rape?

The Desperate Migrant

Home is on fire
No food, no water
Nobody to inspire
Sooner or later
I need to move
And fly like dove

Starvation and hunger
Thirst and boredom
War and dagger
No love, no freedom
America or Europe
Asia, I throw my rope.

Sell the land or house
Borrow, I will pay tomorrow
Though you eat mouse
I will stop your sorrow,
Let me go and return
None again will mourn

A lonely track I meet
Desert only, the set
Choked in car engines
Sliced by plane blades,
I jumped skyscrapers
I climbed fences
Tangled in barbed wire

Bitten by snakes
Chased by animals
I drink urine
I eat feces
I sleep on the tree
In the thick forest
Survival of the fittest

I get raped
I get robbed
I get shot
I get ambushed
I get killed
I get suffocated
I get drowned
I get murdered
I get strangled
I get stabbed
I get eaten
I get jailed
I get tortured
I get whipped
I get buried
I get forgotten

The Mississippi Slave

Angrily, papa sold me
Hungrily, ate my proceed
Submissively, mama could not see
Obediently, again she did bleed.

Bound with the heaviest of chains
Dragged across the shores
Beaten beyond bearable pains
Bruised, broken, inflicted with sores.

Naked all through winter
Lonely, in and out of season
Starved, until summer
Laboured above any reason.

Forced to hang my brother
Alone dug his grave
Made to sleep with my sister
Faced the turbulent wave.

One by one, I laid the bricks
I worked more than the ox
Daily I had many strokes
I lived in a box

Fallow

If we plant sorrow
Today or tomorrow,
Then we must borrow
To fill the hollow,
For the torment under our pillow
Can never go low
Even if we drive below
Without saying hello
To our fellow,
Though we turn yellow
And grow narrow
We cannot maintain the furrow
By leaving it FALLOW

The Government

There is a movement
For thorough improvement
Tagged "development
Against underdevelopment"
But there is an allotment
That is an impediment,
It brings argument
Rather than augment,
This is not a sentiment
Neither is it a detriment,
Watch the tournament
It tears the ligament
And fades the pigment,
Without any rudiment
It ends in bereavement
Which becomes the wonderment
As a general implement;
None should miss merriment
Nor the national enjoyment
Because any can ferment
And also foment
Letting loose the firmament
Under any agreement,
There is a requirement
For every assignment,
It should not be astonishment
How one gets retirement,
Rather a refreshment
Yielding from entertainment,

Instead of disappointment
In place of appointment
Because disagreement
Within the regiment,
Can soil the management
And boil mismanagement
To destabilize the government

A B C D
(Alliteration)

Alice Annoys Amanda And Angela
Blessings befalls beyond beliefs
Charles's Cry Causes Chief's Calmness
Dennis Denies Doing Dirty Deal

Emelda Exhibits Eunice's Elegance
Felix Fights Fever Fiercely
Godwin Greatly Goes Green
Hearing Henrietta, Henry Hid Here

Israel Is In It Independently
Jackson Joins John Judiciously
Kane Kills Kind Kenyan King
Love Leads Life Like Light

Mark Meets Margaret, Marries Mary
Nancy Needs Naomi
Overcomers Order Oranges
Pranks Piss Peace Personally

Queen Queries Quarks
Rose Runs Rat Race
Stephen Says Something Sensible
Teaching Teaches The Teacher Too.

Understanding Uncovers Untold Umbrella
Victor Violates Vulnerable Viola
Watch While Waiting
X-ray Xenophobia

Yearning Yields Yellow
Zambian Zombie Zooms Zebra

I inherited it incredibly

Similar Difference

I will not hit the nail
On my own nail,
And travel to Turkey
To eat a fat turkey,
Because what I saw
I cannot cut with saw

If I be a minor
And do something minor,
I may not bend
When I get to the bend,
Because I can kill a fly
And still always fly.

When I put my foe to flight
Then I can take a flight
When I erect the post
Then I can Mann my post,
When I clean my face
I can then read the face.

When I go to book
I can read my book
Nothing is at stake
Except I hang on the stake,
Reading the sentence
May not be a sentence.

If I look able

I may not be able,
If I am single
I may not work single,
If I dream great
I may not be great.

The courage I summon
Is not a summon
My beautiful ring
Is not a wrestling ring,
If I open the scroll
I can still scroll.

Brainwashed

Born without a choice
Fed with only rice,
Groomed without the chalice
Taught to be an apprentice.

I will take you to the city
Where there is purity,
There, you will be a king
To you, all men, will sing.

I will take you to Italy
There, dwells harmony,
You will know no poverty
There, lives reality.

I will wear you a bomb
So that you visit the tomb,
Kill more than a thousand
Then enjoyment; you understand.

I will give you a coat
So become a he-goat
I want a hundred children
Impregnate even the chicken.

Go, rape a foetus
Then you will be a man
Go, kill your brother, Justus
Then, I buy you a van

Our ancestors told me so
Our grandfathers knew,
Anyone you fail to do
Your strength, you cannot renew.

Yearly, feed me with blood
Quarterly, give me human flesh
Always, open the gates of flood
Let my spirit swim afresh.

I am called mystery
None has my mastery
If you disobey; misery
Because I inflict mockery.

You are brainwashed
Because I am whitewashed
We are sandwiched
And we are finished.

The Irony

The criminal; the prosecutor
The wolf; the shepherd

The friend; the enemy
The lover; the hater

The saint; the Satan
The angel; the Lucifer

The helper; the killer
The preacher; the butcher

The colleague; the saboteur
The leader; the beheader

The reality; the irony

Marriage Nothing but a Responsibility

With the wrong perception
We dwell in misconception,
Shying away from preparation
And diving into miscalculation,
Marriage, nothing but a responsibility

Make up your mind
Never to lag behind
As you gather and find
Together you shall rewind,
Marriage, nothing but a responsibility

Care is a necessity
Love is a duty,
Affection; not in pity
Sex; not an atrocity,
Marriage, nothing but a responsibility

Peace is the beam
Unity is the stream
Both are a team
Together, they pursue a dream,
Marriage, nothing but a responsibility

None should be a donkey
None must be a monkey,
The two must be a key
Then, none would be lanky,
Marriage, nothing but a responsibility

Forget it, if he speaks lies
Then, he attracts flies
As she laments and cries
He stinks more and dries,
Marriage, nothing but a responsibility

A Manager

On the hot seat
To see if I could beat,
More fire and heat
To know if I would cheat,
Raw and bloody; the meat
To watch me come out neat,
Weird and cruel the treat
But God is near for the feat

Short or long my finger
My prayer must linger,
Deep and dark the danger
I am not any stranger
Someone born into the manger
Descended as a messenger
He made me a passenger
And promoted me to A MANAGER

Return Young Chibok

Chibok, my little angel
You were forced to the brothel
Denied the place of education
Made to live in rejection
Taught to sleep with snake
And fed with soured cake

Chibok, you have seen hell
No soothsayer can ever tell
I wonder about the red flag
And how you carry the tag
It is not even their business
Instead it gives them happiness

Chibok, bored and traumatized
Cajoled, tortured and dramatized,
Locked up, imprisoned, dozing
Lonely, moody and losing
Troubled within and without
Yet you dare not shout

Chibok, the ray of greatness
Rose, trampled in the wilderness,
Back home, papa is done
Mama is dead and gone
If you ever come back
Who would serve you a pack?

Help Dear Lord

They are fighting for a crown
Blowing up the whole town
Burning our wedding gown
Turning everything brown,
Putting everyone down
Believing it makes them renown
Help! Help! Dear Lord, we drown

Dirty are they, not golden
Our dreams, they have stolen
Our homes, they have broken,
Hidden in their coven
Tortured on their oven
Reasons, not to be given
Help! Help! Dear Heaven

Goodluck

Hit hard the knock
Break off the padlock,
Never be under lock
Move on with the pluck,
Goodluck to Chibok

We know how you buck
With or without any sock
Calm, like a bullock
Yet severally they struck,
Goodluck in Chibok

Be strong like a rock
Look away from the guck
March on for Chibok
With God, it is chock
Goodluck, dear Goodluck

Castigated and criticized? Move on
Condemned, compromised? Fight on
Discouraged, disappointed? March on
Remember, from nothing, you won
These shall inspire your son.

There Is God

We all are imperfect
It is a clear subject
However, there is a simple fact
Which makes a huge impact
Very undisputable, there is God

Gravity cannot pull Him down
Even when we all frown
Though life is full of fears
And we are afraid of tears,
Yet unerasable, there is God

Troubles bring us to our feet
There, anything we can meet
Sometimes, not that we are bad
Not also that we are mad,
Most believable; there is God

Nigeria is moving forward
Never to be wayward
Incomprehensible; we are moving
Incredible; we are sowing
Concur, I still, there is GOD

Heed

Reside where you can provide
Decide on your bride
Hide not by the side
Ride to bring pride.

Tide can grow wide
Abide and take a stride
Chide and also confide
Glide but never slide

Courage when troubles rage
Damage not at your age
Storage is good for the sage
Blockage rejects a new page

Bondage is equal to cage
Stage produces some wage
Mortgage does not really engage
Passage is the time of voyage

Listen

Charm is likely to harm
Arm yourself in the farm
Balm has to be warm
Storm fears no swarm

Light up your flight
Fight with all your might
Right l and be bright
Night is not too tight

Fed and constantly overfed
Led astray to the bed
Sped away as they fled
Red, the blood, they shed

Mark can be the clerk
Dark does not reveal a mark
Shark never can bark
Park may harbour an ark.

Hearken

Jubilate, if you have a date
Calculate and think of fate
Reciprocate and never be late
Inculcate rather than hate

Celebrate, lock not the gate
Appreciate even if not your mate
Rate and make things accurate
Debate and save your state

Procrastinate, you may castrate
Emancipate, rather than abate
Relate everything in the crate
Terminate evil, lest they dilapidate

Germinate, do not infiltrate
Educate, let none be illiterate
Discriminate not, never segregate
Congratulate and eat from the plate

Lean On the Rock

Blame can bring shame
Frame can also hinder fame
Game can make one lame
Name, unchanged remains same

Sin makes one not to win
Pin kicks you into the bin
Grin and laugh with your chin
Tin is not some gin

Nature makes one to mature
Suture brings a posture
Gesture can work with stature
Culture sometimes leaves a fracture

Unlock and roll away the block
Stock and gather for the mock
Knock and mingle with the flock
Pluck and lean on the rock

Stay Alert

Cast not your hope on the past
Mast up and be vast
Fast to avoid new blast
Last, be strong and steadfast

Gold is not good to be sold
Hold it and never fold
Cold can never make you bold
Told, there is a lot to unfold

Match your dreams on your watch
Catch up with your batch
Hatch and also patch
Scratch not the latch

Place your prayers not in displace
Grace showered, no more disgrace
Face up and score a brace
Race on and dominate the space

The Boundary

Mockery is a form of battery
Flattery can perform some surgery
Penury can never be sugary
Sanitary includes being monetary

Rivalry differs from roguery
Mystery can decode misery
Treachery pollutes legendry
Strawberry can make it slippery

Literary works are more imaginary
Ordinary become extraordinary
Binary can be learnt at plenary
Rosary said by sundry

Piggery does not match fishery
Eatery is not luxury
Thuggery goes with robbery
Necessary always is the boundary

No Kicking Like a Ball

Here, everyone is a role player
Inside or outside the layer
There, is one, a great payer
He may not be an undertaker
This makes me feel safer
Though not a soothsayer
Fervently, I say my prayer

A lot, gives me happiness
It affects also my boldness
In, I feel the consciousness
Though out, much distress
Here and there, deep stress
Around, trouble and mess
But sure, God has my dress

Nature has a true package
It may not be on the stage
Even when hidden in a cage
Painted on a dirty page
Strangled under a rage
Paid a very wrong wage
Just to limit your age

Rejoice, God knows it all
He will not allow the fall
Instead, you, He will call
Lifting you high and tall
Building around you a wall
Extending you like a hall
Then, no kicking like a ball

Some Toke

I live in the Ghetto
My food is potato
My cream is tomato
As I imagine the Kilimanjaro
Fly pass me, the flamingo

My friend lives in the slum
He drinks nothing but rum,
Sometimes, he can go for gum
Not that he likes the sum
But because he has no Mum

I think about complacence
It looks like confidence
And appears like pretense
It may have a little of innocence

Someone suffers from stroke
He is about to choke
Let another be there to poke
Instead of cracking a joke
And giving him some toke

Never You Be Sold

I hate pulling me by force
Instead, allow me to reinforce,
Because if I have every resource
I may withdraw the source

Allow me to give you my best
Just drop the request
Stamp it on my chest
I will pass the test

Every man is gifted
In order to be lifted
So never have them shifted
Mostly, if they are spirited

Write with pen and paper
Talk to a helper
Give to the needy and pauper
God is the only rewarder

Let not fear put you on hold
With no blanket under the cold
And none to make you bold
Do not fold, NEVER YOU BE SOLD

Home

A place of peace
And true love,
A place of unity
And warmth,
Home, the abode of angels.

Intruders are resisted
Trespassers, warded off
Enemies are subdued
Scavengers barricaded
Home, the dwelling place of God.

East, west, north or south
Far, near, up or down,
In, out, low or high
Rich, poor, sick or sound
Home is just God.

Nature

Nature, your air so calm
Healing like balm,
Your water is pure
Great like cure,
Your grass is green
Just like teen,
Nature your land is love
With showers from above
Your sound is loud
Without a bound
You are so unique
So real, so beautiful
Nature, you are a god.

Chains

On our hands are chains
Tying us from winning
On our legs are chains
Stopping us from moving.

These chains are heavy
They weigh us down
Our prayers go up
Transcending forces
But these chains chase them.

Political chains, religious chains
Social chains, societal wounds
National chains, cultural chains
They terrorize, they traumatize
Chains, heavier than earthmoving machines.

Slavery

The old devil lives
He dies not,
The ancient goddess roars
Searing, severing, polluting.

Black on black, black on white
White on black, white on white
He would not just go away.

Poverty, ignorance, illiteracy
Indoctrination, initiation
Deceit, lies and greed
Slavery, enslaving us.

Modernization and civilization
Rebranding and upgrading
Enhancing and enticing
Slavery, shinning better.

Relatives selling out
Friends buying in
Counterparts gaining all
Rivals, challenging more.

Greed

Old mockers join together
Young dreamers flee away
Cruel models distort lanes
Vulnerable followers get lost.

Greed is all they cook
They steam it as creed,
Feed raw their might
Fight real for their breed.

This greed is epidemic
They write as epistle
And seem episcopal
But they are the Apocalypse.

Hate

They hate so passionately
Unfortunately without a cause
They plant deep a curse
And throw away the cross
Because they hate the course.

We yearn and yawn
We long in lack
And linger in want,
Yet they care not
Because they hate us.

Humans trading humans
Exchanging them for gold
Giving them for oil,
Humans, so desperately wicked.

Their hate is satanic
They fold up in barbarity
And spread atrocity,
These ones are demonic.

Vengeful, hateful,
Monstrous, cancerous
Ridiculous, callous, poisonous
Corrosive, we wail, we cry, we weep
Yet, nothing ever changes.

Humanity

Humans are gone
None does exist
Humans are lost
None does live.

They killed humanity
And acquired inhumanity
They looted godliness
And kept ungodliness
They sold governance
And bought wickedness,
Humanity exists no more.

Ask them, they can testify
Yes, they know all is gone
Life is crazy, love is madness
Lust rules them, lies leads them
Deceit and mischief defend them
Humanity murdered itself.

Men hate their maker
They challenge him
Men question they creator
They doubt him,
Men abuse their God
They put him to flight,
Humanity is on crossroads.

about the author

Ngozi Olivia Osuoha is a Nigerian poet, writer and thinker. A graduate of Estate Management with experience in Banking and Broadcasting.

She has published six poetry books and co-authored one (with Amos O. Ojwang').

She has featured in more than forty international anthologies and also has published over two hundred and fifty poems and articles in over twenty countries.

Many of her poems have been translated and published into other languages, including Spanish, Romanian, Khloe, Farsi, and Arabic, among others.

She has won many awards; she is a one time *Best of the Net* nominee, and she has numerous words on marble.

CPSIA information can be obtained
at www.ICGtesting.com
Printed in the USA
BVHW081219170619
551189BV00004B/873/P